Where's my DOGGY?

First published in Great Britain 2022 by Farshore
An imprint of HarperCollins*Publishers*
1 London Bridge Street, London SE1 9GF
www.farshore.co.uk

HarperCollins*Publishers*
1st Floor, Watermarque Building, Ringsend Road
Dublin 4, Ireland

Illustrated by Hannah McCaffery
Additional images Images used under license from Shutterstock.com

This book is an original creation by Farshore
© 2022 HarperCollins*Publishers* Limited

ISBN 978 0 0084 9477 3
Printed in Italy
001

A CIP catalogue record for this book is available from the British Library.

MIX
Paper from
responsible sources
FSC™ C007454

This book is produced from independently certified FSC™ paper
to ensure responsible forest management.

For more information visit: www.harpercollins.co.uk/green

Contents

Theme Park Pups 20-21

Best in Show 22-23

Tasty Treats 24-25

Sports Day 26-27

Doggy Marathon 28-29

Kennel Chaos 30-31

Did You Know? 34-35

More to Find! 36-39

Answers on p32-33

Meet the Dog Pack

These five doggy friends are ready for adventures! Spot them in all the busy scenes in this book.

Mango the Jack Russell

Mango is the big boss of the dog pack. He likes to lead all the other dogs into mischief.

Molly the Cockapoo

Molly is a champion hole digger. You can usually spot her by looking for the trail of holes.

George the Sausage Dog

George is a sleepy sausage dog. If there's a patch of sun to nap in, that's where George will be.

Bert the Labrador

Bert loves nothing more than playing at the park. He is an expert stick-catcher.

Rex the French Bulldog

Rex is a hungry pooch and his big ears can hear a treat packet open anywhere. They do make it hard for him to hide though.

Beach Bonanza

There's no better place for a digging-loving doggy than the beach! You'll find Molly digging a hole in the sand. Can you spot the rest of the dog pack, along with these hidden items?

5 blue buckets

3 Collie puppies

3 dogs snorkling

Palace Pooches

The Royal Corgis are having a party at the palace and all the pups are invited! See if you can find Mango and his friends as well as these extras hidden within the scene.

5 Corgis　　3 horses　　1 crown

Cute Canines

These miniature breeds are super cute and perfect to curl up in your lap. Can you spot the pack hiding among their little pals?

Winter Wonderland

The dogs are having a brrr-illiant time playing in the snow! Look out for cheeky Bert carrying a snowman's arm. Can you find the pack in this snowy scene along with these items?

3 snowmen

2 sleighs

1 igloo

SNOW CONE ←

HOT SOUP

SKI LIFT →

PUPPUCCINO
SOLD HERE
→

15

Puppy Parlour

These pampered pooches are having a day at the parlour. With a shampoo and a trim, they'll look fabulous in no time! Along with our five pups, can you find these beautiful breeds?

5 Poodles 4 Dalmatians 3 Afghan Hounds

Huge Hounds

These gentle giants are the biggest dogs on the block. Can you find our pack hidden among them?

Theme Park Pups

These thrill-seeking dogs are having a wild ride at the theme park. Can you find the gang in the crowds along with these hidden items? Even some sneaky cats couldn't resist joining the fun!

1 clown

3 dog shaped balloons

5 cats

Best in Show

It's the biggest day in every dog's calendar - show day! Only the best breeds will rise to the top and swipe the big prize. Look for our five pups along with these talented pooches.

4 perfect Poodles

3 speedy Greyhounds

2 sleepy Basset Hounds

Tasty Treats

Rex is a peckish pooch who can hear a packet of treats opening from a mile away. Can you spot him and the rest of his hungry friends hiding among these yummy treats?

Sports Day

There's an activity to suit every pup at Sports Day ... except perhaps George, who would much prefer a nap! Can you find him and his friends, as well as these extra items?

A St. Bernard sleeping

10 broken eggs

3 rosettes

Doggy Marathon

Ready ... set ... race! The dogs are running a marathon as the crowds cheer them on. Can you catch our pack among their speedy friends? See if you can spot these extras too.

A Newfoundland asleep

A trophy

5 blue flags

28

Kennel Chaos

After a busy day getting up to lots of mischief, it's time for these tired-out pups to have a nap. Can you spot our sleepy gang among these cosy kennels?

Answers

Beach Bonanza

Palace Pooches

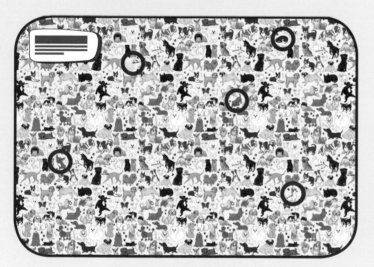

Cute Canines

Winter Wonderland

Puppy Parlour

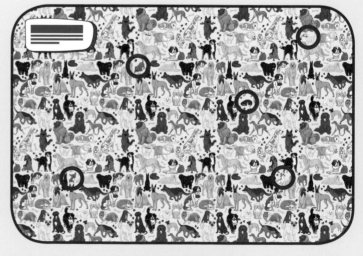

Huge Hounds

Theme Park Pups

Best in Show

Tasty Treats

Sports Day

Doggy Marathon

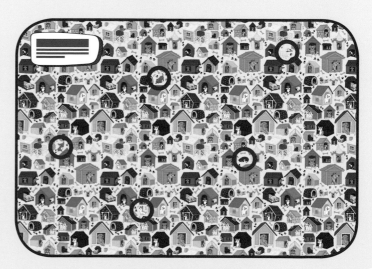

Kennel Chaos

Did You Know?

Tennis Balls

A Golden Retriever called Finley broke the world record for holding 6 tennis balls in his mouth. Now that's a good boy!

How Long?

A St. Bernard called Mochi won the world record for being the dog with the longest tongue in the world - measuring 18.58cm. That's one slobbery dog!

Whoosh!

Greyhounds are the fastest dog breed and can run as fast as 45 miles per hour. Watch out when these dogs get the zoomies!

So Cute!

The smallest dog breed is the Chihuahua with an average height of just 15-23cm. Well they don't call them a toy dog for nothing!

"Hello Up There!"

The tallest dog breed is the Irish Wolfhound with an average height of 81-86cm. Despite their enormous size, they are super friendly.

More to Find!

Now you have found all our fluffy friends in the book, go back through and complete these checklists to discover other fun finds!

Beach Bonanza

- ( ) A dog windsurfing
- ( ) 2 dogs wearing shark fins
- ( ) 3 dogs with fishing rods
- ( ) 2 dog lifeguards
- ( ) A Dalmatian playing volleyball
- ( ) 2 dogs stealing a string of sausages
- ( ) A dog reading a newspaper
- ( ) 2 dogs taking pictures

Palace Pooches

- ◯ The Queen
- ◯ Dalmatian puppies having a picnic
- ◯ A brass band
- ◯ A dog flying a kite
- ◯ 2 dogs wearing sun hats with flowers
- ◯ A Collie with 3 hoops in its mouth
- ◯ A dog wearing a royal cape
- ◯ A group of dogs playing lawn bowls

Winter Wonderland

- ◯ 2 snowdogs
- ◯ A Dalmatian snowboarding
- ◯ A Chihuahua making snow angels
- ◯ A Great Dane wearing green earmuffs
- ◯ 4 dropped ice creams
- ◯ 3 German Shepherd puppies
- ◯ 2 dogs playing tug of war with a scarf
- ◯ A Poodle asleep under a red blanket

Puppy Parlour

- ◯ A dog with a punk hairdo
- ◯ 3 dogs with green gift bags
- ◯ 2 red bowls of bones
- ◯ 3 dogs having pedicures
- ◯ 2 dogs sweeping up
- ◯ A dog with a big green bow
- ◯ A lady carrying pink towels
- ◯ A Pug in a bathrobe

Theme Park Pups

- ◯ A dog floating with balloons
- ◯ A man dressed as a hotdog
- ◯ A Bulldog with 3 drinks
- ◯ A dog with a blue hoop
- ◯ A lady with candyfloss
- ◯ A yellow bone balloon
- ◯ A Shih Tzu with an ice cream
- ◯ 5 purple doughnuts

Best in Show

- ◯ A Collie jumping through a hoop
- ◯ 2 security guards with red clipboards
- ◯ A trophy
- ◯ A black dog with a yellow rosette
- ◯ A ballerina
- ◯ 2 bouquets of flowers
- ◯ A dog doing a handstand in a top hat
- ◯ A red bucket of bones

Sports Day

- ( ) A St. Bernard limboing
- ( ) 2 dogs howling
- ( ) 3 green hula hoops
- ( ) A Poodle skipping
- ( ) A Pug about to win the sack race
- ( ) A dog waving two flags
- ( ) 2 blue buckets of eggs
- ( ) Some dogs doing a three-legged race

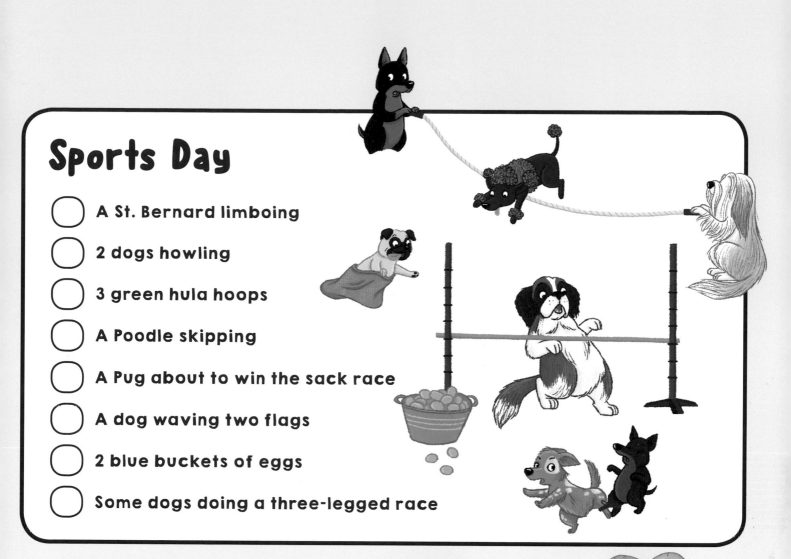

Doggy Marathon

- ( ) A Poodle dressed as a bone
- ( ) A dog wearing a green cape
- ( ) A Husky howling from a window
- ( ) A dog holding 2 red flags
- ( ) Number 30 lying down
- ( ) A Schnauzer digging a hole
- ( ) A boy holding a bone sign
- ( ) A dog taking a photograph